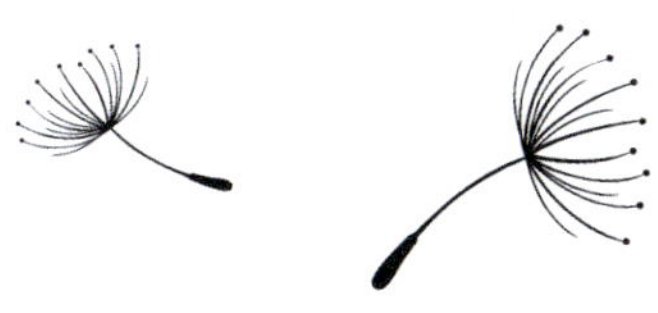

Seeds

by Rachel Russ
illustrated by Natalie Vasilica

OXFORD
UNIVERSITY PRESS

Lots Of Seeds

Look at the seeds!

See lots of seeds with me!

Seeds With Wings

This is a common weed.

If you puff it, the seeds sail up.

This seed zips along on its wings.

Then it dips.
It is in the mud.
It will be a seedling.

Seeds With Hooks

This seed
has hooks.

hook

It hooks on
to a dog.

The dog runs.
Off pops the seed.

Oak Seeds

Look at this big oak.

Look!
Lots of oak seeds up high.

The oak seed has a seed coat.

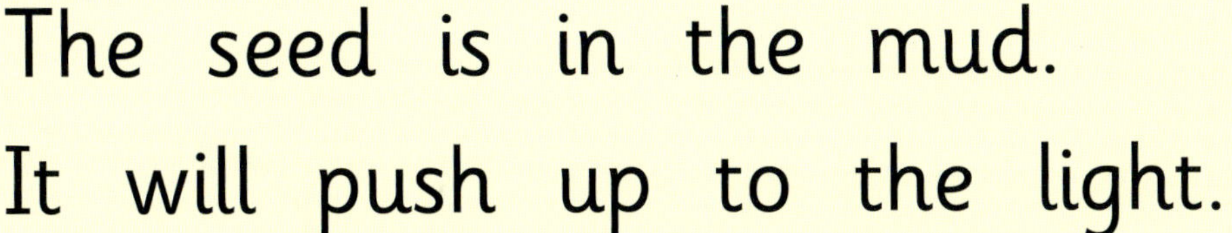

The seed is in the mud.
It will push up to the light.

Seeds need to be wet.
Seeds need the sun.

Then the seed will be a seedling.
It will be an oak.

Encourage students to match the seed to the plant.